Uncle Johnson

Uncle Johnson,
The Pilgrim of Six Score Years

By

REV. GUSTAVUS L. FOSTER

UNCLE JOHNSON, THE PILGRIM OF SIX SCORE YEARS.

BY

THE REV. GUSTAVUS L. FOSTER.

Philadelphia
Presbyterian Board of Publication
Printed in 1867

Uncle Johnson

REMEMBER YOUR WEEKLY PLEDGE
" Upon the first day of the week let
every one of you lay by him in store, as
GOD hath prospered him." The Apos-
tle Paul's charge to the Corinthians.
1 Cor. xvi. 1.
TO THE MASS.
A.S. SOCIETY.

Uncle Johnson

Uncle Johnson

Uncle Johnson

11

UNCLE JOHNSON,
THE PILGRIM OF SIX SCORE
YEARS.

Uncle Johnson

Uncle Johnson

IT is still the custom in some towns of the West, as well as in New England, to announce the death of individuals by measured strokes of the bell, each stroke marking a year of the life of the dead. This practice, though originating in superstition, the ringing of the bell being held as efficacious for the driving away of evil spirits, in its continuance is not without profit.

Many can testify to the blessed influence of such announcements. Many can remember the thoughts and purposes that were inspired thus--whether the solemn tones fell upon their ear at early morn, telling that one had passed through the valley of the shadow of death during the night, or whether they were heard just as evening's lengthened shadows, or the hush of twilight's hour made them impressive. It is well that thus, amid the hurry and strife of life, mortals shall be made to pause and think whither they are tending.

Not long since the inhabitants of Y --, wearied and wondered in counting the strokes of the bell, as the iron-tongued accountant told first the numbers of infancy, then of childhood, then of manhood, then of old age, and still tolled on in a number

beyond even old age. But the wonder --
"Who has died?" passed away ere the
counting had reached one hundred and
twenty, telling the number of the years of
some ended pilgrimage. All knew that
"UNCLE JOHNSON"
had at last gone home.

Since his departure, we have thought of
many things concerning that venerable relic
of a former generation, things of so much
interest to us that we are constrained to tell
them to others. He was one of our most
intimate neighbors for years, living in a
humble cabin upon a lot, which joined the
back end of our own. From our study-
window, we could look down upon his
garden, and in the summer season, we had
no difficulty in being familiar with the tenor
of his life.

Before "Uncle Johnson" came to dwell
in the cabin it changed its occupants
frequently, and at each change, we were
glad and hopeful. Hearing that the place had
now been purchased by a colored man,
though free from any special prejudice

against his race, our hopes on the score of good neighborhood were not raised high. [1]

We soon found that we were subject to no annoyance from the cabin; that all was quiet and orderly there. We heard little except that at times more frequent than morning and evening the voice of praise and prayer ascended with a peculiar fervor from within its walls. Listening once to these sounds, we heard these words: "O Lord, dy servant has been a pilgrim more dan a hundred years, when will he get home?"

Such a declaration induced us to think that our new neighbor might be both an aged and good man. At any rate it led to an intimate acquaintance in which we found that in both of these respects he was a man most rare.

By frequent conversations concerning his age, we judge that his death occurred in his one hundred and twentieth year.

---

[1] He was of purely African descent. His full name was Johnson Harrison--the Harrison, as he said, being his master's name in Virginia, and the Johnson his own. For this reason, he preferred being called Johnson.

Uncle Johnson

His first master felt that his servants were in some sense members of his family, and recorded their names in the family Bible. The old man remembered seeing opposite his name 1745. The month he could not recall. In confirmation of the great age, which such a date would give him, as he lived to the year 1864, he said that he was a man grown when sent out to throw fireballs in the evening because of the joyful news of the signing of the Declaration of Independence. Concerning the events of the revolutionary war, so far as they occurred upon the line of the James' River, Virginia, he was familiar. General Washington was frequently at his master's house, and his master was a member of the first Assembly. He said: "De last time I seed de General 'twas when de war was ober. I bated de General's horse in de yard, while he takes dinner wid de masser."

He stated also that he was about thirty before he was allowed to have a wife; that he lived with her fifty years; then for several years had no wife, and his last wife, who died two years before him, said that she had lived with him twenty-eight years. He also stated that he was set free by his last master and sent to Canada, partly because he was more than one hundred years old, and by right of age deserved to be his own man. He delighted in telling of the scenes of his early life, and his narrations would so accord with the pages of history as to make it evident that he had lived as far off from the present as he asserted. Certainly, he was a wonderful man as an "ante-revolutionary relic."

But he was still more interesting and wonderful because of his religion. He accounted for his long life in part by saying: "I neber worked bery hard. When I was a boy I chored 'bout house, and den for about sixty years I blowed de gospel trumpet on de plantation for 'bout six months ob de year, to make de slaves good and 'ligious, and I tell ye, massa, when I was in my prime, say along 'bout eighty, I could blow de old trumpet so dat dey could hear me for miles." His own account of his early religious knowledge and experience was about as follows:

"I was quite a chunk of a boy afore I hearn much about 'ligion, afore I hearn much about dis glorious gospel.

"Once in 'bout a year one o' dem clergy dat com'd ober de big water com'd round and preached up all de funerals ob de slaves dat died sen he com'd afore, and sometimes I feels very bad den. But after a bit dere com'd round one ob de big men from de college in de Jarseys, and he told us 'bout de matter werry solemn. But I know nothing den about Jesus." And now the tears began to trickle down the old man's cheeks. [2]

"An' den dar com'd along dat man dat died an' den com'd to life again, an' he told de slaves 'bout Jesus. Oh, wat was he name? I don't mind now." I suggested William Tennent. "Oh, yes, massa! Willie Tennent! Glory to God! I been tryin to tink ob dat name dese many years. I knowed I should know him in glory, but now I will call him by name jus as soon as I sees him. After I heard him how I did feel! Wen I was walking on de ground it would keep sayin' 'Unworthy! unworthy!' Wen I took a bit ob bread, or a cup ob water, dey keep sayin' 'Unworthy! unworthy!' Wen I goes into de field all de trees keep sayin' 'Unworthy! unworthy!' Wen I goes into de yard I sees dat all de cattle kneels down afore dey lies down, an' I neber done dat. O massa, I thought I should die. I feels so bad." (Then he would go on in various terms to tell of his

---

[2] This it seems probable was the eloquent President Davies.

utter despair.) "But bimbye dere com'd along a colored man who told me des no use in my libin' dat way. He telled me ob de passage dat says: 'Behold de Lamb of God dat takes away de sins ob de world;' an' den I goes into de woods, an' all night I cries, 'O Lamb of God, hab mercy on dis poor man;['] an' I cries an' prays dis ober an' ober; an', O massa! just as de light was coming ober de mountains ob ole Virginia de light of Jesus shined into dis poor soul, an' from dat day on, now about a hundred years, I've been tryin' to tell to saints and sinners round what a dear Saviour I have found."

He was ever magnifying the grace that rescued such a sinner as he, and that had sustained and comforted him in his long and weary pilgrimage. We have never known one whose soul would so soon melt and flow down in the presence of the great facts of infinite love and mercy. The name of Jesus was the greatest and best of all names to him. Not unfrequently, he would utter that dear name over and over, with tones, and tears, and gestures of gratitude and praise.

The old man was favorably situated for enjoying ejaculatory worship; and he diligently improved and richly enjoyed his opportunities. For about five days in each week he was alone in the most of the day; his wife, who was sixty years younger than himself, having gone out to work in neighboring families, and his two children, born after he was one hundred years old, having gone to school or to play. During their absence he would often spend hours in talking, and praying, and singing. Sometimes, as one of my children said, he appeared to "play meeting." Sitting in his chair by the side of his house with his Bible on his knee he would slowly read (without glasses) and expound and preach as if a congregation were present; then would follow singing and prayer in a manner which would indicate that Christ himself were present. We called upon him one day just as he closed one of these services. As soon as he saw us he cried out, with tears flowing down his face: "O massa! Jesus has been here, an' I tought I was in glory; but I will be dere bimbye."

"You mean to be faithful to the end, Uncle Johnson?" I said.

"O massa, I'se bound for de kingdom. I'se not been holding on all dis way to fail jus at de gate."

Once, as I interrupted him upon one of these occasions, he exclaimed:

"O massa! de Lord is passing by; does you want to speak to him?"

I can call to mind many interesting incidents concerning him, but will mention only a few of such as made the most impression upon my mind at the time. His voice and manner were such as to give his declarations a power that they cannot have upon the lifeless page. The reader needs to imagine his earnest manner and emotional utterance with the tone common among preachers and exhorters at the South many years ago. The fact, too, that he did not appear to know that he had said anything interesting when he had uttered thoughts as rich as human language can express, gave to his words a peculiar charm. They would come forth as spontaneously as if they were the natural outflow of his soul, as if they were specimens of the rich quarry within, or as if God would thus show what can be wrought in a heart that gives him entire dominion.

One day while he was at work in his garden, singing and shouting, I said: "You seem happy to-day."

Uncle Johnson

"Yes, massa, I'se jus tinking."

'What are you thinking of?"

"Oh I'se jus tinking;" (and then his emotions prevented utterance.) "I'se jus tinking dat ef de crumbs dat fall from de Master's table, in dis world, am so good, wat will de GREAT LOAF in glory be! I tells ye, massa, dar will be nuff an' to spare dare."

At another time when he seemed very happy and I had heard him shout, "Lord Jesus, will dere be one for me?" I said, "You are having a good time to-day, uncle?" He answered:

"O massa, I was meditatin' about Jesus bein' de Carpenter; an' so he can make mansions for his people in glory." And then with uplifted face and with tears he cried out, "O Jesus, will dar be one for me?"

Once I said to him, "Uncle Johnson, why don't you go to church once in awhile?" He answered, "Massa, I wants to be dere, but I can't 'have."

"You can't behave?"

"Well, massa, you knows, late years, de flesh be weak; an' when dey 'gins to talk and sing about Jesus I 'gins to fill up, and putty soon I has to holler, and den dey say, 'Carry dat man to de door, he 'sturb de meetin'.'"

"But you should hold in until you get home."

"O massa, I can't hold in--I bust if I don't holler."

Once, after hearing him pray and sing at midnight while a thunder-storm was passing, in the morning I said, "Was that you shouting so last night?"

"Yes, massa, I 'spose."

"Well, I thought the thunder made noise enough without your hallooing."

He looked up, and with astonishment said: "Massa, do you tink I'se goin' to lie dere on my bed like a great pig, wen de Lord com'd along shakin' de earth and de heavens? No, massa, when I hears de thun'er coming, I says, 'Ellen, Ellen, wake up here, we's goin' to hear from home ag'in.' "

One morning when I had heard him for an hour or two, I went carefully to his door and saw him sitting at the end of his table with a humble repast before him, while his hands were lifted high in gratitude and praise. I said, "You seem happy this morning?"

"Oh, yes, Ellen went away to her work, and so I gets me breakfast and den begins to say grace; an', O massa, de Lord am so good, seems I neber will be done sayin' grace!"

What a rebuke to those who sit down to loaded tables with no thought of their Benefactor!

Gratitude to God for his daily mercies was one of his most distinct peculiarities. If he received a gift from his neighbor he ever evinced an appreciation of the kindness of the giver; and then, at once, his eye would be lifted toward heaven, and some expressions would clearly indicate his heart's response to Him from whom we receive every good and perfect gift. Many things, received from time to time, were regarded by him, and spoken of as if they came in answer to prayer. He said, "When I wants anything I asks de Lord, and he's sure to send it, sometimes afore I done asking, an' sometimes he waits jus to see if I trusts him."

Once when we indicated a little skepticism upon this subject, he said:

"Massa, don't you know dat de Lord send de ravens to feed de prophet? Him is jus as good now as den."

We chanced to be present when one called with whom he was not acquainted. After entering and shaking the old man by the hand, he said: "Is this Uncle Johnson? I have often heard of you, and have meant sometime to see you. But as I was passing just now something said to me, 'Go in there and give the old man a dollar.' I said, 'I can't do it;' and again something said: 'Go in there, I tell you, and give him a dollar.' So here it is, get anything you please with it."

"Yes, massa, thank you, thank you. I tought de Lord would send you dis afternoon. Sit down, sit down."

"No, not now, I am in a hurry. I hope you are getting along comfortably. Good-bye."

"Hold! hold! Massa! Afore you go I wants to know if you are bound for de kingdom? May-be I'll neber see you again. Am you bound for dat land of pure delight, where saints immortal reign? Hab you de passport?"

"The what?"

"De passport all signed and sealed wid de blood of Jesus. You must hab dat, massa, or you neber will get fru de gates ob de city."

In some such manner as this he would improve every opportunity of doing good to those who came in his way. He would with perfect naturalness run all conversation into a religious channel. "Out of the abundance of the heart the mouth speaketh." He was perpetually saying such things as declared plainly that he was seeking a country, that is, an heavenly.

His anticipations of the heavenly inheritance were such that at times he thought himself in full possession. Said he: "Sometimes when I'se walking up and down in dis cabin, praising de Lord, I thinks I am in heaven; I thinks dis is one ob de mansions dat Jesus gives his people. Den dis world is

under my feet. I jus sees it a great way off,
and I jus cries: O my God! am I in glory?"

"But how do you feel when you find
that you are not there?"

"I has a long crying, and den I says, I
will wait my appointed time."

"How long would you be willing to
wait?"

"I will wait anuder hundred Years, if de
Lord please."

Realizing his need of fitness for heaven
we heard him praying one night: "O Lord,
anoint our souls with angels' balm, that
when we have done with dis world we may
be at home in glory."

His voice was so strong and his soul so
fervent that he was heard in his devotions
for a great distance around, especially at
evening, in the season of summer. Many
were necessitated to hear the accents of
prayer and praise, though themselves never
uttered them. Some persons doubtless were
annoyed by this, and yet in various ways
they would indicate their approbation of his
manner of life. Many a wicked man laid

himself down and rested all the more quietly, by reason of the sense of safety inspired by the prayer he was compelled to hear, before retiring; and many a one was waked to the active duties of a new day by the early praises of this aged pilgrim who seemed to welcome each coming morning as bringing him nearer home.

He uniformly rose early, but especially early on the Sabbath. When we asked him why he did so he said: "De Lord get up early dat day. De women dat went to de sepulcre got dere early, and den de Lord was not dere. De earlier I gets up de more I sees ob Jesus."

By reason of his infirmities he could not attend upon the services of the sanctuary, but said he: "I puts up for you ebery day; I always pray den for all dat blows de gospel trumpet."

Nothing rejoiced him more than to hear that sinners were inquiring the way to the Saviour. Such tidings would make him weep for joy. Once, lifting his hands, he cried: "O Lord, call dem in. Ho Lord! Make dem willing in de day of dy power."

Uncle Johnson

Once, in illustrating that sinners should
be more in earnest, he said: "Many tink dey
be seeking and seeking 'ligion, and dey be
jus putting it off all de time; dey must lay
right down to it, jus as de hos would to de
dray, or dey neber can get free. You know
de gate is narrow -- 'tis mighty narrow!"

His confidence in the word of God was
unbounded. Let him be sure that the Lord
had said anything, and nothing could shake
his faith in it. We were mentioning this fact
to a friend one day just as we were going
over to call on the old man. So, after having
been there a while, my friend said:

"Uncle Johnson, you believe so and
so," naming some fundamental doctrine of
the gospel.

"Yes, massa, I believes dat."

"What makes you believe that?"

"'Cause, massa, you knows dat de Lord
says so," quoting a passage or two.

"Well, Uncle Johnson, you believe so
and so," (naming another doctrine,
seemingly antagonistic to the former.)

"Yes, massa, I believes dat, too, 'cause de Lord said," and then he quoted again.

"But see here, uncle, both of those things can't be true; you said you believed so and so, and also so and so. Now how do you reconcile these two things? They can't both be true, in the nature of things; it is not philosophical that both should be true." And thus my friend went on attempting to confuse the old man with metaphysical subtleties.

Uncle Johnson heard him for a while, and then lifting himself from his chair, and in a manner indicating grief and impatience, said:

"Massa, I knows nothing about your philosophies and your natur ob tings, but I knows dat de Lord said dem tings, an' I hab tried de Lord more dan a hundred years, (weeping,) and I'se not going now to gib up one ting dat he said."

Having said this he sat down. My friend turned and said to me, in a low tone: "That will do; I give it up."

He seemed to have so long rested upon the simple declarations of God, and to have had so many fulfilments of the promises in his own experience, that anything intimated or said in a manner indicating distrust of these things was regarded with no degree of allowance. It seemed hard for him to believe that a man can be a Christian and indulge in any measure of skepticism concerning anything that is clearly revealed. For "the philosophies of religion" he cared nothing. Its grand and glorious facts were great enough and rich enough for his capacities. He had a confidence in God so strong as to believe that there are good reasons for all his assertions, and that he need not trouble himself with an endeavor to look into them. Oh! how well it would have been for many if they had been like poor old Uncle Johnson! Very few know enough to make it worth while to be curiously inquisitive of divine secrets. Simply to trust is the most profitable way of learning the things of the divine kingdom. God makes his most blessed revelations to those who most completely confide. This we often thought when staggering home under the weight of some of Uncle Johnson's simple but almost inspired utterances.

But while we were marking the general tenor of that life of faith and prayer, we gave it a new attention, as it revealed itself, under the chastenings of affliction. A great sorrow overtook him in the death of his wife, about two years before his own release. She rapidly but very trustfully went into the valley of the shadow of death. Returning from an evening appointment we were told that she was dying. Hastening over we found that the spirit had just taken its departure, and then we saw and heard what we can never adequately describe. What a figure of grief and triumph in the presence of the stillness and solemnity of death!

This aged one, standing by the bedside of the lifeless form of his wife, with uplifted face and hands, was crying: "Farewell, Ellen -- farewell, my dear Ellen; must you leave me! must you leave me! O Jesus! my dear Ellen is coming! Gib her one ob de mansions till I come; Lord Jesus! How can I wait? Send de chariot again."

Such like expressions were numerous until the tide of his emotions had subsided; then, kneeling by the bedside, he breathed his sorrows into the ear of his Saviour in such a prayer as we never expect to hear again.

From that hour on, through the funeral occasion and in the days following, his spirit and manner were beautiful beyond description. Being human he often felt lonely, and believing that he would ultimately attain heaven, he greatly longed to be there. We said to him one day:

"Uncle Johnson, don't you feel lonely since Ellen left you?"

"Oh yes, massa, I feels berry lonely, but den de Lord comes round ebery day and gives me a taste ob de kingdom, jus as de nus would wid de spoon; but, oh! how I wants to get hold ob de dish," (suiting the manner to the words.)

Ever after Ellen's death he seemed only waiting as he said "for dat chariot to come again." Once, after he had been ill for a few days, as he began to get out again, I said: "I thought that your appointed time had about come." He replied: "Oh, yes, I tought dat day dat I could see de dust ob de chariot coming ober de mountains, an' den somethin' said, 'Hold on, Johnson, a little longer; I'll come round directly.' Yes, massa, an' I will hold on, if de Lord please, anoder hundred years! for I'se bound for Canaan." Then he broke out singing:

"But this I do find we two am so jin'd,
  He'll not live in glory and leave me
behind."

During those days he would often bid
his friends farewell, "till we meets in glory."

One day the Rev. Dr. H -- called on
him with me. After a conversation which,
surely my friend will never forget, he said:
"I must now go; good-bye, Uncle Johnson;

I shall probably hear soon that you have
gone over Jordan, but we will follow on."

"Oh, yes massa, great many years ago
young men like you tell me dat, an' den after
a bit I'd hear dat dey had gone home, an' I
am a pilgrim yet, but I always manages to
send word."

"Well if I should die first," said Dr. H -
-, "what word would you send?"

"O massa, if you get home afore I do,"
(weeping,)"tell 'em to keep de table standin',
for Johnson is holding on his way. I'se
bound to be dere."

Uncle Johnson

We might record other incidents and expressions, but they would be like those already given. Many who have visited him, and who may see these pages, will wonder that we have not told of what he said when they were present. We have narrated only such things as made the deepest impression upon our own mind, and which we have retained by notes made at the time, or by repeating them.

Since the death of his wife the old man has been almost wholly dependent upon his neighbors for daily bread. Those women who have ministered to his comfort, or more distant friends who have supplied his wants, will not lose their reward. They have been already rewarded in having had an interest in the prayers of this man of God.

Uncle Johnson fasted and prayed as very few in these days have done. His fasting, as well as praying, were thorough and earnest. For more than seventy years he entirely abstained from food on Fridays. He said, "Dem am de days wen I says to do body'stan' back dere; I'se going to feed do soul today.'" When I asked, "Don't you sometimes feel very weak and faint before night?" he said, "Yes, massa, but den I must have de body keep he place." In speaking of these days of fasting and prayer he once said: "Dese are de days when I spreads de big tings afore de Lord and begs."

Of his death we know but little. His illness was brief. In such an hour as he thought not the Son of Man came. But that he was ready when "the chariot" came, and that "its wheels rolled in fire," as when Elijah was born to heaven, we may not doubt.

As we have marked this old man's life it has often seemed as if "one of the prophets had risen again." He had a faith like that of Abraham, a firmness like that of Daniel, a fire like that of Isaiah, tears like those of Jeremiah, and he fasted and prayed like them all. We rejoice in having known such a man, and in having seen in him so many of the excellent things of the kingdom of God. He was a living witness of the power and glory of the gospel of the blessed God. Often looking on him have we asked, "What would this aged African have been but for the divine plan of elevating and saving men?" And then again we have asked, "If it doth not yet appear what we shall be, what will he be ages hence?"

Grace has its wonders. God is yet choosing the weak things of the world to confound the mighty, and it will be seen more distinctly by-and-by than now, that there are first which shall be last, and last that shall be first. Nothing but simple trust in Christ can endure man with true greatness. Little child-likeness goes before, and is essential to the stature of a perfect manhood.